A COLLEGE ALBUM

Gaudeamus igitur,
Jùvenes dum sumus;
Post jucundam juventutem,
Post molestam senectutem,
Nos habebit humus.

Alma Mater floreat,
Quæ nos educavit,
Caros et commilitones,
Dissitas in regiones
Sparsos congregavit.

Spring on the Yale campus: the class of 1886 poses as freshmen for an informal picture beneath the elms that line the "Old Brick Row." *O, fortunati, O terque beati!* (as the song goes), these are the gilded youth of their age.

Two great Harvard professors, the naturalist Louis Agassiz and the mathematician Benjamin Peirce, in 1871.

Two earnest students at Hiram College,
Ohio, in 1852: future President James A.
Garfield (right) and William Boynton.

6

What would be the "image" of education for women? Vassar solved the riddle with its graduation-day daisy chain. One got on it for attractiveness *and* good marks and good works. This 1900 chain certainly qualifies on the first requirement.

To grasp the gulf in college manners between past and present one need only study for a moment this elegant young Harvard man, James Nichols, amidst the sentimental clutter of his room in 1892. The only low note is struck by the spittoon.

INVENIEMVS VIAM AVT FACIEMVS

The pictures for this book were assembled from many archives, as credited, by Carla Davidson, assisted by Devorah K. Cohen. The design and typography are by Ulrich Ruchti and the copy-editing by Carol Angell. I should like to thank E. M. Halliday, my long-time collaborator in editing American Heritage magazine, and Kenneth Leish, General Manager, American Heritage Book Division, for reading the manuscript, and Murray Belsky, Editorial Art Director of this company, and Kaari Ward for their help.

The front endpaper shows an otium-cum-dignitattery of young Methodists in their room at Wesleyan College, Middletown, Connecticut, about 1870, and comes from the Culver Picture Service in New York; the back one displays a Betty-Co-Eddery of pretty students at the University of Wisconsin in 1939, the heyday of the saddle shoe, and appears here through the courtesy of the State Historical Society of Wisconsin.

Library of Congress Cataloging in Publication Data Jensen, Oliver Ormerod, 1914–. A college album. 1. Universities and colleges — United States — History — Pictorial works. I. American heritage. II. Title. LA226.J43 378.73   74-11045   ISBN 0-07-032457-3

A COLLEGE ALBUM

BY OLIVER JENSEN
AND THE EDITORS OF AMERICAN HERITAGE
THE MAGAZINE OF HISTORY

CONTENTS

PUBLISHED BY
AMERICAN HERITAGE PUBLISHING COMPANY, INC., NEW YORK

BOOK TRADE DISTRIBUTION BY
McGRAW-HILL BOOK COMPANY

FOREWORD

On hearing of the plan to found what would become, in 1636, Harvard College, John Winthrop's sister Lucy rushed him an encouraging note. "I beleev a colledg would put no small life into the plantation," she wrote in the carefree spelling of the time. In the inelegant argot of ours, she said a mouthful. Out of that puny, earnest, and pious beginning has grown the lumbering, stumbling, yet aspiring industry we call higher education, with its 2,600-odd colleges and universities, some great, some small, and some odd indeed, and its current enrollment of just under nine million scholars. Giantism, egalitarianism, and a touching faith in the perfectability of any institution are hallmarks of this country, and we have approached learning as though it were a canal or a transcontinental railroad or an oil field: throw in enough people and enough money and it will work.

The news that comes to us today of this educational juggernaut is disturbing, a series of crises identifiable simply by listing a few recent vogue-words: "nonnegotiable demands," "antielitism," "pass-fail," "open admission," "black studies," "antiparietalism." Violence on the campus has ebbed but left behind it a general loss of faith, standards, and sense of direction. Sometimes the only clear message that reaches us from Academe is a call for funds, and that on a staggering scale. As an example, Yale is seeking from its often disenchanted alumni an additional endowment of $370,000,000—twenty-four times the cost of the Louisiana Purchase. On the other hand it is less than one seventh the cost of Skylab; matters of relative value are hard to sort out in these fast-moving times. And one might bear in mind also that it is bad news, generally speaking, that makes the front pages, not the untroubled campus, not the successful professor, not the hard-working and able student.

Against this tumultuous background we set our book of photographs, with their wonderful power to evoke the past as it actually was, or at least that revealing fragment that the camera selected. It is not in any sense a full history but a visit, beginning roughly in the middle of the last century, two centuries after Harvard began, one after the painful curriculum laid out in the advertisement shown opposite. It starts when the earliest practical photographs are available, a period bounded by *"Gaudeamus"* (which can be translated as "Let us rejoice" or "Live it up," depending on one's period) on the one hand and "Puff, the Magic Dragon," with its veiled allusions to drugs on the other. We have called on about one hundred college archives and our own picture files at AMERICAN HERITAGE magazine to show the life and times of the American undergraduate; we are most grateful to all the patient archivists who have helped us, even though we have been forced by limited space to omit many fine pictures. If our selection of photographs seems subjective or less than truly representative of various colleges and activities, we plead guilty to letting the best pictures take charge. To us they seem to prove Lucy's prophecy correct. And they seem to establish as well two apparently opposite truths, that revolution is constant on the campus yet that students themselves never really change.

The PENNSYLVANIA GAZETTE.

Containing the Freſheſt Ad- ---- *vices, Foreign and Domeſtick.*

To the PRINTERS of the PENNSYLVANIA GAZETTE.

BY Order of the *Truſtees*, we ſend you the following PLAN OF EDUCATION, now fixed by them for a *three Year's Trial*, in the LATIN, GREEK, and PHILOSOPHY SCHOOLS, of the *College and Academy* of this City; by a bare Inſpection of which, any Parent may know what Progreſs his Son makes, and what is his Standing, as well as what Books to provide, from Time to Time. The *Plan* of the *Engliſh School*, and the *School* for the *practical Branches of the Mathematics* will alſo be laid before the Public as ſoon as poſſible.

Philadelphia,
College and Academy-Hall, Auguſt 5, 1756.

WILLIAM SMITH, *Provoſt of the College and Academy.*
FRANCIS ALISON, *Vice-Provoſt of the College, and Rector of the Academy.*
EBENEZER KINNERSLEY, *Profeſſor of Engliſh and Oratory.*
THEOPHILUS GREW, *Profeſſor of the Mathematicks.*
PAUL JACKSON, *Profeſſor of Languages.*

A VIEW of the LATIN and GREEK SCHOOLS, on their preſent Plan.

1ſt STAGE. Grammar. Vocabulary. Sententiæ Pueriles. Cordery. Æſop, Eraſmus.
N. B. To be exact in declining and conjugating. To begin to write Exerciſes, for the better underſtanding of Syntax. Writing and Reading of Engliſh to be continued if neceſſary.

2d STAGE. Selectæ e veteri Teſtamento. Selectæ e profanis Authoribus. Eutropius. Nepos. Metamorphoſis. Latin Exerciſes and Writing continued.

3d STAGE. Metamorphoſis continued. Virgil with Proſody. Cæſar's Comment. Salluſt. Greek Grammar. Greek Teſtament. Elements of Geography and Chronology. Exerciſes and Writing continued.

4th STAGE. Horace. Terence. Virgil reviewed. Livy. Lucian. Xenophon, or Homer begun.
N. B. This Year to make Themes; write Letters; give Deſcriptions and Characters. To turn Latin into Engliſh, with great Regard to Punctuation and Choice of Words. Some Engliſh and Latin Orations to be delivered, with proper Grace both of Elocution and Geſture. Arithmetic begun.

Probably ſome Youths will go thro' theſe Stages in three Years, many will require four Years, and many more may require five Years, eſpecially if they begin under nine or ten Years of Age. The Maſters muſt exerciſe their beſt Diſcretion in this Reſpect.

Thoſe who can acquit themſelves to Satisfaction in the Books laid down for the fourth Stage, after public Examination, are to proceed to the Study of the Sciences, and to be admitted into the College as Freſhmen, with the Privilege of being diſtinguiſhed with an Under-graduate's Gown. The Method of Study to be proſecuted in the College for the Term of three Years, follows in one general View.

A VIEW of the PHILOSOPHY-SCHOOLS.

	FORENOON. INSTRUMENTAL PHILOSOPHY.		AFTERNOON. CLASSICAL and RHETORICAL *Studies.*	PRIVATE HOURS. MISCELLANEOUS STUDIES.
FIRST YEAR.	LECTURE I.	LECTURE II.	LECTURE III.	*For improving the various Branches.*
FRESHMEN. *May 15.* *Firſt Term.* Three Months.	Latin and Engliſh Exerciſes continued.	Arithmetic reviewed. Decimal Arithmetic. Algebra.	Homer's Iliad. Juvenal.	Spectators. Ramblers and monthly Magazines, for the Improvement of Style, and Knowledge of Life.
Second Term. Three Months.		Fractions and Extrac. Roots. Equations, ſimple and quadratic. Euclid (*Stone*) ſix Books.	Pindar. Cicero. Select Parts. Livy reſumed.	Barrow's Lectures. Pardie's Geometry. Maclaurin's Algebra. Ward's Mathematics. Keil's Trigonometry.
January. *Third Term.* Four Months.	Logic with Metaphyſics.	The ſame a ſecond Time. Logarithmical Arithmetic.	Thucydides, or Euripides. Wells's Dionyſius.	Watts's Logic, and Supplement. Locke on Human Underſtanding. Hutcheſon's Metaphyſics. Varenius Geography.
Remarks.	*N. B.* At leiſure Hours Diſputation begun. Duncan's Logic as a Claſſic; to be ſupplied by *Le Clerc*, or Crouſaz on Syllogiſms.	*N. B.* On Conſtruction of Logarithms, uſe Wilſon's Trigonometry, and Sherwin's compleat Tables by Gardiner.	*N. B.* Some Afternoons to be ſpared for Declamation this Year.	Watts's Ontology and Eſſays. King de Origine Mali, with Law's Notes.
SECOND YEAR. JUNIORS. *May 15.* *Firſt Term.* Three Months.	Logic, &c. reviewed. Surveying and Dialling. Navigation.	Plain and Spherical Trigonometry.	Rhetoric from Preceptor. Longinus, critically.	Voſſius. Boſ. Pere Bohours. Dryden's Eſſays. Prefaces. Spence on Pope's Eſſay. Trapp's Prælect. Poet. Horace. Demetrius Phalereus. Alluſiones.
Second Term. Three Months.	Conic Sections. Fluxions. *Ditton's.*	Euclid, 11th Book. 12th Ditto. Architecture, with Fortification.	Horace's Art of Poetry, critically. Ariſtot. Poet. critically. Quintilian, ſelect Parts.	Patoun's Navigation. Gregory's Geometry. Biſſet on Fortification. Simpſon's Conic Sections. Maclaurin's and Emerſon's Fluxions. Palladio by Ware.
January. *Third Term.* Four Months.	MORAL PHILOSOPHY *begun.* *Viz.* Fordyce's compendious Syſtem.	NATURAL PHILOSOPHY *begun.* *Viz.* Rowning's—Properties of Body, &c. Mechanic Powers. Hydroſtatics. Pneumatics.	COMPOSITION *begun.* *Viz.* Cicero pro Milone. Demoſthenes pro Cteſiphon.	Helſham's Lectures. Graveſande. Cote's Hydroſtatics. Deſaguliers. Muſchenbroek. Keil's Introduction. Martin's Philoſophy. Sir Iſaac Newton's Philoſophy. Maclaurin's View of Ditto. Rohault per Clarke.
Remarks.	*N. B.* Diſputation continued. Fordyce well underſtood will be an excellent Introduction to the larger Ethic Writers.	*N. B.* Declamation continued. Rowning as a general Syſtem may be ſupplied by the larger Works in the laſt Column, recommended for private Study.	*N. B.* During the Application of the Rules to theſe famous Orations, Imitations of them are to be attempted on the Models of perfect Eloquence.	
THIRD YEAR. SENIORS. *May 15.* *Firſt Term.* Three Months.	Hutcheſon's Ethics. Burlamaqui on Natural Law.	Rowning on Light and Colours. Optics, &c. Perſpective. *Jeſuit's.*	Epicteti Enchiridion. Cicero de Officiis. Tuſculan Quæſt. Memorabilia Xenophontis, Greek.	Puffendorf by Barbeyrac. Cumberland de Leg. Selden de Jure. Spirit of Laws. Sidney. Harrington. Seneca. Hutcheſon's Works. Locke on Government. Hooker's Polity.
Second Term. Three Months.	Introduction to Civil Hiſtory. to Laws and Government. to Trade and Commerce.	Aſtronomy. *Keil's.* Natural Hiſtory of Vegetables. of Animals.	Patavii Rationar. Temporum. Plato de Legibus. Grotius de Jure, B. & P.	Scaliger de Emendatione Temporum. Compends in Preceptor. Le Clerc's Compend of Hiſtory.—Gregory's Aſtronomy.—Forteſcue on Laws. N. Bacon's
January. *Third Term.* Four Months.	Review of the Whole. Examination for Degree of B. A. *N. B.* Altho' it is thought neceſſary to fix ſome Claſſics as a Text to read the Lectures by; yet there muſt be a Liberty of changing them left, when needful.	Chemiſtry. *Shaw's Boerhaave.* Of Foſſils. Of Agriculture. *N. B.* Thro' all the Years, the French Language may be ſtudied at leiſure Hours.	Afternoons of this third Term, for Compoſition and Declamation on Moral and Phyſical Subjects.—Philoſophy Acts held.	Diſcourſes. My Lord Bacon's Works. Locke on Coin, Davenant. Gee's Compend. Ray. Derham. Spectacle de la Nature. Rondolethus. Religious Philoſopher.—HOLY BIBLE, to be read daily from the Beginning, and now to ſupply the Deficiencies of the Whole.

This formidable document exhibits both the strengths and weaknesses of American eighteenth-century college learning; the Bible will "supply the deficiencies." Founded in 1753, this became the University of Pennsylvania.

IN THE BEGINNING

Although in our times any wide place in the road with more than one building is apt to call itself a university, higher education in the American colonies was not modelled on the great universities of late medieval Europe, those societies of masters and scholars that sprang up in Paris and Bologna, freely organized places without buildings, laboratories, endowments, rules, or outside activities. (They had plenty of inside activities, so to speak, within the minds of the scholars.) Our early colleges descend from seventeenth-century England, which was riven by religious battles between Puritans and established church. As many as seventy-five of the emigrant Puritan "saints," as they modestly described themselves, or over half of all the college graduates, had been to Emmanuel College, Cambridge, where the new faith had established itself. And the plantation in the Massachusetts Bay Colony was but sixteen years old when, as the author of *New England's First Fruits* put it: "One of the next things we longed for, and looked after was to advance *Learning,* and perpetuate it to Posterity, dreading to leave an illiterate Ministry to the Churches when our present Ministers shall lie in the Dust." Within two years a Cambridge graduate named John Harvard left the infant institution about £780 and some three hundred books, and thus bestowed his name on what is now our great-

est university. (Appropriately enough, a Boston-born Welshman who had made a fortune in the East India Company at Madras, Elihu Yale, achieved the same immortality at the second greatest for a more modest £550. He never saw his college.)

Sectarianism among the Protestants was a powerful force. The second college founded, for example, William and Mary in 1693, was intended to produce Anglican ministers for Virginia. After a promising start, which included the creation there in 1776 of Phi Beta Kappa, it suffered during the Revolutionary era from war and its backing by the Anglicans, who were closely identified in the public mind with the Tories. It was occupied by everyone from Lord Cornwallis to (much later) the Union Army, and has been closed three times.

The third foundation was Yale's in 1701; it was originally called a collegiate school, and it wandered about Connecticut from Saybrook to Killingworth and eventually to New Haven, a town that made an offer of land that the ten Harvard-trained ministers who founded it could not refuse. To some extent Yale owed its existence to a conservative reaction against Harvard, where distressing liberal religious tendencies early began to manifest themselves. Indeed, Harvard's first president, Henry Dunster, was removed from office for questioning infant baptism. It would be only a step from that to atheism (which most of the Harvard students professed by the 1790's) or even Unitarianism, which pretty well took over in the early nineteenth century. Perhaps that grim Trinitarian Cotton Mather smelled it coming, because it was he who persuaded

LAWS,

RELATING TO THE

MORAL CONDUCT, AND ORDERLY BEHAVIOUR,

OF THE

STUDENTS AND SCHOLARS

OF THE

University of Pennsylvania.

1. None of the students or scholars, belonging to this seminary, shall make use of any indecent or immoral language: whether it consist in immodest expressions; in cursing and swearing; or in exclamations which introduce the name of GOD, without reverence, and without necessity.

2. None of them shall, without a good and sufficient reason, be absent from school, or late in his attendance; more particularly at the time of prayers, and of the reading of the Holy Scriptures.

3. Within the walls of the building, none of them shall appear with his hat on, in presence of any of the Professors or Tutors; or, in any place, fail to treat them with all the respect which the laws of good breeding require.

4. There shall be no playing in the yard, or in the street, during the time in which the schools are assembled; nor, within the walls of the building, at any time: nor shall any boy cut or notch the furniture of the rooms; or draw any figures or characters on the walls; or tear, deface, or in any way injure, the books, or other property, belonging either to himself or others.

5. When the schools are dismissed, whether in the morning or afternoon, the boys shall not remain in the yard, or in the neighbourhood of the building; but shall immediately disperse without noise or tumult, and return each to his respective home, so as to be at the disposal of his parents, or of those under whose care he is placed.

6. The students of the Philosophical classes shall, each of them in succession, deliver an oration every morning in the Hall, immediately after prayers; the succession to begin with the senior class; and, in each of the two classes, to proceed in alphabetical order.

7. In case of the transgression of any of the above laws, the transgressor, if he belong to either of the Philosophical classes, or be above the age of 14 years, shall, for each transgression, be subject to a fine, or suspension; and, if under that age, to the same penalty, or to corporal punishment, at the discretion of the Faculty. The fine, in no case, to exceed 25 cents.

8. And if any student of the Philosophical classes, not prevented by sickness or other unavoidable necessity, shall twice successively neglect to appear in his turn, and pronounce his oration, as above directed; he shall be considered as guilty of a wilful disobedience to the laws of the institution; and shall be suspended, until, recourse being had to his parents or guardians, some competent security can be obtained for his more orderly behaviour in future.

Extract from the Minutes of the Board of Faculty.
WILLIAM ROGERS, *Secretary.*

September 19th, 1801.

LAW

OF

HARVARD UNIVERSITY,

REGULATING THE DRESS OF THE STUDENTS.

April 29, 1822.

THE dress of the Undergraduates shall be as follows:—

The coat of black-mixed,* single breasted, with a rolling cape square at the end, and with pocket flaps; waist reaching to the natural waist, with lapels of the same length; skirts reaching to the bend of the knee; three crows-feet, made of black silk cord, on the lower part of the sleeve of a Senior, two on that of a Junior, and one on that of a Sophomore: The waistcoat of black-mixed or of black; or when of cotton or linen fabric, of white, single breasted, with a standing collar: The pantaloons of black-mixed or of black bombazet, or when of cotton or linen fabric, of white: The surtout or great coat of black-mixed, with not more than two capes. The buttons of the above dress must be flat, covered with the same cloth as that of the garments, not more than eight nor less than six on the front of the coat, and four behind. A surtout, or outside garment, is not to be substituted for the coat.

* By black-mixed (called also Oxford mixed) is understood black, with a mixture of not more than one twentieth nor less than one twenty-fifth part white.

But the students are permitted to wear black gowns, in which they may appear on all public occasions. Night-gowns, of cotton or linen or silk fabric, made in the usual form, or in that of a frock coat, may be worn, except on the sabbath, on exhibition and other occasions when an undress would be improper.* The neckcloths must be plain black or plain white.

No student, while in the state of Massachusetts, shall, either in vacation or term time, wear any different dress or ornament from those above named, except that in case of mourning, he may add the customary badges.

This law shall go into operation at the beginning of the first term after Commencement, viz. the 28th of September next, provided that those students, who are already furnished with clothes, not conforming to the uniform above required, may continue to wear them, on procuring the written request of a parent, guardian, or patron to that effect.

Any student, violating these regulations, and persisting therein after admonition, shall be dismissed from the College.

* Those, who are now provided with cloaks, may wear them, subject to the exceptions annexed to the use of night-gowns.

A little of the flavor of college life in the early 1800's comes through in these documents, with their strict rules of dress and conduct and the strange value system revealed in Amos Clarke's bill from Harvard (which would cost him $5,350 a year today). Fines were levied for all manner of offenses, including tardiness at prayers (a penny, the lowest fine), profanity, lying, picking locks, rudeness, "tumultuous noises," fighting, and "refusing to give evidence" against others. The highest fine was for "tarrying out of town one month without leave" (fifty shillings).

Amos Clarke to the **President** and **Fellows** of **Harvard College** Dr.

To his third Quarter Bill, ending April 5, 1804.

Interest to be paid, if not discharged within three Months.

	Dolls. Cents.
Steward and Commons	16. 48
Sizings	1. 93
Study and Cellar Rent	1. 50
Instruction	4. 50
Librarian	.60
Books	
Catalogue and Commencement Dinner	.55
Repairs	.55
Sweepers and Sand	.36
Wood	1. 50
Seat in the Episcopal Church	.75
Fines	.33
	5
	33. 54

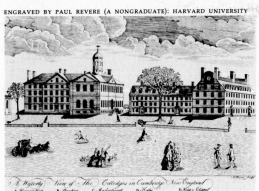

Harvard College in 1767

William and Mary in the early 1800's

Elihu Yale to make his donation to the rival institution. In any case, Yale remained for many years a bastion of Congregational orthodoxy. It fired its third rector, Timothy Cutler, in 1722 for a leaning toward "Episcopacy" and expelled two students in 1744 for going to a revival—with their parents and during vacation!—and it hung on to compulsory chapel for generations after Harvard abolished it in 1886. That interesting Harvard exercise may be observed in our two little cartoons of about 1850, on page 14, drawn by a student and entitled "Morning Devotions."

The revival that proved so disastrous for the two Yale men of 1744 was part of the Great Awakening, led by that persuasive stirrer of souls George Whitefield; it was an emotional religious outburst that filled the colonies, the churches, and the colleges with turmoil as well as what was then called, in a special meaning, "enthusiasm." Out of the more radical faction of Presbyterianism that resulted grew Princeton, chartered in 1746 as the College of New Jersey. Congregationalists were harder to stir up than Presbyterians; Whitefield was not invited to speak at Harvard. But "enthusiastic" Congregationalists backed Eleazar Wheelock in converting his Indian school into Dartmouth College; Baptists also infected with revivalist fervor produced the College of Rhode Island (later Brown), and the Dutch Reformed Church founded an institution in New Jersey called Queen's that in 1825 became Rutgers, after Henry Rutgers, a New York merchant who gave it five thousand dollars.

So it all began. With the addition of faintly Episcopal King's College (later Columbia) in New York—George III hoped it would "guard against total Ignorance" and instill "just principles of Religion, Loyalty and a Love of Our Excellent Constitution," passing it a positively cut-rate £400 at the same time—and of a nonsectarian college at Philadelphia (see page 13) in which that noncollege man Benjamin Franklin played a part,

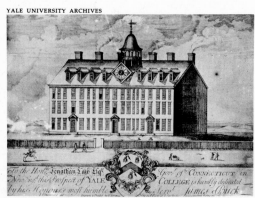

Yale College about 1750

The College of New Jersey, at Princeton, about 1756

The University of California, Berkeley, in 1874

The University of Michigan in the 1870's

there were nine colleges in America at the onset of the American Revolution. Their purposes had long passed the purely religious; they were "private" in their general control despite varying degrees of support from government. They had benefitted spasmodically from government taxes and other oddities of support: Harvard received the income of the Charlestown ferry tolls; Yale was awarded the take from some privateering; William and Mary was assisted by Virginia imposts on tobacco and peltry, and the right to commission county surveyors (among them George Washington). How small these hopeful pillars of piety were in fact can be glimpsed in the pictures opposite; how restrictive by the two "laws" reproduced on page 15. The course was narrow and classical, conducted to no small extent in Latin; in the tradition of the English colleges their small American descendants took seriously their responsibilities *in loco parentis* to young men boarding with them, many of whom were barely into their teens. There was no nonsense about equality, and barely one colonist in a thousand was a college graduate.

That this system produced learned men in both "Church and Civill State," as the founders of Yale put it, cannot be gainsaid, but it was doomed by the progress of American democracy, signalled by the success of the Revolution itself. The aristocratic ideal was dying, like the Federalist Party, in a wave of egalitarian optimism. Even though there were few if any secondary schools to prepare the necessary students, state legislatures, communities, and religious sects began founding colleges everywhere. They were poor and small and lamentably undersupplied with learned men, but they proliferated. Some endured, some failed. Several simply burned down. The most aspiring if not the most secure were in the Middle West and West, stark, bare buildings like those shown on this page, a long way from Harvard, an incalculable distance from Emmanuel College, Cambridge.

The University of South Dakota in 1891

The entire University of Oklahoma in 1892

A PRIMITIVE BROTHERHOOD

"Indulged, petted, and uncontrolled at home, allowed to trample upon all laws, human and divine, at the preparatory school . . . [the American student] comes to college, but too often with an undisciplined mind, and an uncultivated heart, yet with exalted ideas of personal dignity, and a scowling contempt for lawful authority, and wholesome restraint."

If this outcry from an anguished professor sounds like 1974 speaking, it actually comes from Davidson College, at Davidson, North Carolina, in 1855, quoted by Frederick Rudolph in *The American College and University*. Perhaps it is a good description of the young men shown opposite and in the inset below, fugitive images from the good old days at the dawn of photography. Everyone, of course, has his good old days. These are mid-nineteenth-century ones, when the country went into the Civil War with some 250 colleges and universities. By 1885–86, when the great English observer of American institutions James Bryce was collecting statistics for his book *The American Commonwealth*, our government's admittedly imperfect figures listed 67,623 students in 345 establishments "granting degrees and professing to give instruction, higher than that of schools, in the liberal arts." Bryce, a friendly critic, was careful to insert that cautious word *professing*. Perhaps he recalled that Agassiz had called even midcentury Harvard "a respectable high school where they taught the dregs of learning." Of that same era Henry Adams said that "Harvard College . . . taught little, and that little ill." And Henry Cabot Lodge, of the class of 1871, wrote that except for Henry Adams' course in medieval history, "I never really studied anything, never had my mind roused to any exertion or to anything resembling active thought."

"If we define a university," commented Bryce, "as a place where teaching of a high order, teaching which puts a man abreast of the fullest and most exact knowledge of the time, is given in a range of subjects covering all the great departments of intellectual life . . . possibly only eight or nine of the American institutions would fall within the definition. Of these nearly all are to be found in the Atlantic States." It is clear that he most admired Johns Hopkins and the later Harvard, which President Eliot, in a long reign beginning in 1869, later transformed into a great university. It was a man's—or a boy's—world of primitive dormitory living, with its frequent rebellions, hazings, and hellraisings. Of things to come, like organized athletics, "outside activities," Greek-letter societies, a broader curriculum, or a genuine education for women, only the first tentative strivings were then to be seen. Yet life within the ivied walls was not without its charm, as George Santayana observed after a visit to Yale, whose students reminded him of "a sort of primitive brotherhood, with a ready enthusiasm for every good or bad project, and a contagious good-humor."

YALE UNIVERSITY ARCHIVES: 1886

To look the part of a desperado is a yearning that seems to over-
take all college boys at some point. This rakish pair at the
University of Massachusetts, about 1870, are unidentified.

Eastern aristocrats might patronize the "aggies," but the new state agricultural colleges of the West and Midwest were the future of mass democratic higher education. One of the pioneer institutions in this new, practical field was Michigan's, at Lansing, chartered in 1855. Here is its faculty in 1890, short on elegance but long on distinction. Third from the left of those standing is the president, Oscar Clute, and behind him in a derby the

noted horticulturist Levi Taft. Both the greybearded patriarchs made their way into the pages of the *Dictionary of American Biography*. They are William James Beal, seated, an eminent early botanist and conservationist, and Robert Kedzie, a veteran of Shiloh, a physician, and a chemist, who spread knowledge through the West on subjects as diverse as clean drinking water, lightning rods, new kinds of wheat, and railroad-car ventilation.

On the surface the American college scene in the autumnal years of the nineteenth century seems placid and formal, a man's world, as suggested in the Yale surveying class at right, sighting instruments under the watchful gaze of Professor William A. Norton. Such an impression might be reinforced by the picture of the classical scholar buried in his books at far right; this awesome presence, that of a firm opponent of co-education, is Professor Henry Martyn Harman of Dickinson College. (The era was strong on the use of three sonorous names, especially for poets, educators, and even Harman's foes the feminists.) In fact, revolution was stirring. Institutions of higher learning, nine at the time of the Revolution, had multiplied to 345 in a century. Harvard had sixty-two in its undergraduate faculty, largest in the country; and its brilliant, austere president, Charles William Eliot (below), who ruled there for forty years, had installed the elective system. Students might choose all but a few of their courses of study. Imagine! Yale, Princeton, and other private seats of imposed wisdom held back. But not the West, and particularly not the eminent educator shown playing baseball at right below.

22

It was the era of great leaders among college presidents, men of mark like Eliot of Harvard, William Rainey Harper of Chicago, Andrew Dickson White of Cornell, James Burrill Angell of Michigan, Daniel Coit Gilman of Johns Hopkins. Two college presidents, Garfield and Wilson, made it to the White House, and there was talk (perhaps partly begun by himself) of nominating Nicholas Murray Butler of Columbia. One of the most able, certainly, was David Starr Jordan, shown at bat at the left; it is hard to imagine many of his silk-hatted contemporaries in such an informal role. Jordan was the first president of Leland Stanford's new university in California, and its freedom and rise to excellence was largely his work in the years 1891–1913. He was also a noted naturalist, a teacher in almost every field, and a bitter-end peace advocate in 1917, often shouted down by crowds with war fever.

These are five of many snapshots taken at Princeton during his undergraduate years by Erskine Hewitt, of the class of 1891. He was the son of Mayor Abram S. Hewitt of New York, and the grandson of Peter Cooper. Someone equipped him with early Kodaks, including the kind that took round glass negatives, and he had an inborn sense of humor. Not much is known, alas, about the rather languid subjects in the photographs.

The men with baby skeletons are in the Science Museum, and the long drink of water at left must be the tallest man at Old Nassau. It is impossible to characterize any large body of students, but Hewitt's pictures do suggest that the Ivy League colleges, perhaps more than their western counterparts in this long-ago time, provided in many cases merely training for what Nicholas Murray Butler called "the simple profession of gentleman."

A kind of golden glow hangs over this all-male Ivy League world of a century ago. Here is the Brown University bicycle club, capped, cravatted, and ready to leap on their "penny-farthings" about 1887.

The nineteenth century brought to the campus the glee clubs with their Germanic choruses converted into college songs. And it gave birth to the comic songsters like this "Moses in Egypt" quartet at Princeton.

28

In quite another part of the forest, here is a graduating class (taken around 1900 but, alas, unidentified) at mostly but not all-black Howard University. Founded in 1867 by Union General Oliver O. Howard, it became the most distinguished black institution.

AN EARNEST SISTERHOOD

In a moment of curiosity and unconscious cruelty the reverend gentlemen in charge of Yale in 1783 examined one Lucinda Foote, who was twelve, and ruled that she was "fully qualified, except in regard to sex, to be received as a pupil of the Freshman class." And then they closed the door on her because people believed that women were generally inferior intellectually to men. As enlightened a man as President Eliot of Harvard said at the turn of the nineteenth to twentieth centuries that he thought women physically too fragile to stand the pace of college and university.

By that time, of course, the die was already cast. Oberlin College, that Ohio amalgam of puritanism and progressivism, began admitting women in 1837 (it had already received Negroes), followed by Antioch and then, one after another, by the growing state universities of the West. Back East had appeared the women's college, like Mount Holyoke, founded in the same year as Oberlin by Mary Lyon, a determined young schoolteacher who raised $27,000 to do it. Her seminary was, at the beginning, little more than a high school educationally (so indeed were many male institutions optimistically called colleges), but a true college appeared in 1861 when Matthew Vassar, a successful brewer, endowed one at Poughkeepsie. Vassar Female College, it was called at first, and the prospectus was careful to point out that the sphere of women was "to refine, illumine, purify, adorn—not to govern or contend." But "male" subjects were taught, and gathering both confidence and skill, Vassar soon dropped what was to feminists the shameful adjective in its title.

The rest of the so-called Seven Sisters soon followed: Mount Holyoke, fully grown to college status; Bryn Mawr under the redoubtable Martha Carey Thomas, one of the first women graduates of Cornell, who shortened her name to a mannish M. Carey Thomas; Smith by a man who intercepted a $400,000 bequest that an heiress named Sophia Smith—who was no feminist at all—was about to give to Harvard; Wellesley by an eccentric man of wealth who hoped it would employ no men at all; and Barnard and Radcliffe. The latter two were, like a number of other "annexes," dependents of male universities.

RADCLIFFE COLLEGE: 1899

UNIVERSITY OF CHICAGO: 1942

Betty Co-ed and her once-cloistered sisters now number over 40 per cent of the nine million American college students. Even though the greater part of this degree-bearing feminine phalanx must at some later date fill in a blank on the alumnae questionnaire with the embarrassing occupation of "housewife," that revolution is over. The next one, which is already well along, was the subject of a remarkable prophecy by M. Carey Thomas in 1898: "The need for separate colleges for women," she said, "separate education for men and women, cannot ultimately prevail. It is a mad waste of educational endowments . . . a madder waste of scholarly power . . . At the close of the twentieth century it will seem absurd."

Girls proved apt imitators of men in the ways of collegiate life. The four young women at right combine a weakness for doughnuts with the traditional freshman beanies. Attempts were made to find a feminine equivalent of the word "freshman," among them "protomathian" at Elmira and "novian" at Rutgers, but these ideas died along with such proposed degrees for women (collected by Daniel Coit Gilman) as "Laureate of Science," "Maid of Philosophy," and "Mistress of Polite Literature." The four in the picture are at pious, Lutheran-sponsored Gustavus Adolphus College in Minnesota, founded during the first great wave of Scandinavian immigration. But the girls below at Reed College in Oregon, cheering a tug-of-war team, are no less earnestly full of school spirit than any pennant-waving Eli in the height of the Bulldog era. Of course, some critics on the outside worried about what the girls were learning, well illustrated in a story quoted by Frederick Rudolph in *The American College and University*. A proud daughter tells her father, "I have made 100 in algebra, 96 in Latin, 90 in Greek, 88½ in mental philosophy and 95 in history; are you not satisfied with my record?" Her father replies, "Yes, indeed, and if your husband happens to know anything about housekeeping, sewing, and cooking, I am sure your married life will be very happy." All of this kind of humor, and genuine worry that women would lose their charm (and marriageability), seems as far away as the Stone Age when set against our time, when women demand to be everything from policemen to actual combat infantrymen.

This idealized photograph of Smith girls on a
stairway of Dewey House was taken in 1904; it is
no doubt how the Amherst boys thought of them.

At top is an 1890 design class at M.I.T., which was co-educational almost from the start. Below, girls take tea in their room at Barnard, 1900.

36

Bryn Mawr was all brains, Vassar all politics and radicals, or so went an old stereotype. Smith was, in that litany, all health and normality, and here go some of its girls for an outing on Mountain Day, in 1905, on a trolley flatcar filled with hay, the only men the motorman and conductor. Today girls bike.

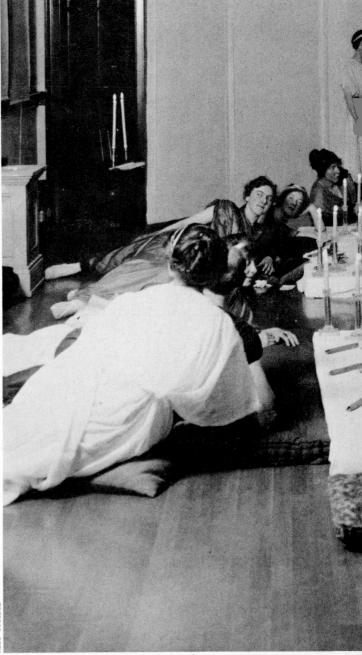

Should there be dancing at women's colleges? Would refinement fly out the window? But once the process was started, it was inevitable that Beowulf and Tennyson would bring on Shaw and Freud, and that "deportment" would give way to "self-expression." Here is the genre in full flower at two progressive women's colleges on the West Coast. The wood sprite of 1918 above and the puckish bacchantes of the 1923 "Vine Dance" opposite above are at Mills in Oakland, California. The large scene at right shows the 1915 Classical Club of Reed College in Portland engaged in a Roman banquet. This was called bringing history to life, but it somehow lacks the snap of the kind of event that amused Caligula, Claudius, and, say, Messalina.

MILLS COLLEGE

40

If opponents of higher education for women worried about their possible loss of femininity and charm, it is perhaps because they did not foresee what is called, in capital letters, The Dance. Here is a sample: May Day at the University of Montana, undated but from a student album running from 1918 to 1922.

NOW THEN, GENTLEMEN

What was it they came to learn, to win the prized degree, and what was the teaching like? Only long memories can recall the old classroom, its musty air, the shuffling feet, the imposing presence on the dais, the round of recitation conducted almost like a catechism. And no living memory can bring back the formal curriculum based mainly on Latin, Greek grammar, mathematics, "Christian evidences," and what were called moral and natural philosophy. There was a little surveying and natural history, recalled in the small pictures on this page (we cannot identify the bone). Only a few pioneers dreamt of a university in its ancient investigative role; in America—unlike Europe—the universities and colleges were petty despotisms, ruled by strong though often brilliant and dedicated men. Most of them meant to preserve knowledge as an accepted body of facts and skills and to pass the cup on to the educated and governing classes of the future. It could be stultifying, especially in the earlier times when everything was conducted in Latin, including the Greek and Hebrew and the ordinary business of the day. It was a dog Latin, to be sure, and the rule was often broken. One of the forgetful old presidents of Harvard, noting a stray dog at vespers, called out, "*Exclude canem, et* shut the door." One stern Yale preceptor, who was wont to reject all excuses with "*Ratio non sufficit*" ("The reason will not suffice"), one day called the name of a student of whose recent death he had not learned. "*Mortuus est,*" someone else answered. "*Ratio non sufficit,*" mumbled the old gentleman.

OHIO STATE UNIVERSITY: 1895

In his book *The Art of Teaching,* Gilbert Highet, one of few brilliant classicists of our time, cites a story that may help explain why the ancient languages lost their pre-eminence. It is William Lyon Phelps's account of his class in Homer when he was at Yale in the early 1880's. Did the teacher seize the opportunity to bring Homer, his age, his plots and characters and importance, to life? No. Instead,

The instructor never changed the monotonous routine, never made a remark, but simply called on individuals to recite [i.e. to translate] or to scan [i.e. to read the verse metrically], said "That will do," put down a mark; so that in the last recitation in June, after a whole college year of this intolerable classroom drudgery, I was surprised to hear him say, and again without any emphasis, "The poems of Homer are the greatest that have ever proceeded from the mind of man, class is dismissed," and we went out into the sunshine.

As for Homer, so for Cicero. In his *Early Cornell,* the late Morris Bishop tells of a Harvard professor who introduced his class to a German Cicero scholar who had spent fifty years in discovering that "while *necesse est* may be used either with the accusative and infinitive or with *ut* and the subjunctive, *necesse erat* can be used only before *ut* with the subjunctive." And he told them seriously, "I should think it well worth living for to have made that discovery." To get a bachelor's degree from Harvard, James A. Garfield observed in 1867, a man "must apply years of arduous labor to the history, oratory, and poetry of Greece and Rome; but he is not required to cull a single flower from the rich fields of our own literature."

"Now then, gentlemen, watch closely!" Before a blackboard listing of landmarks in the history of the uses of steam stands Professor Charles F. Himes of Dickinson College. He instituted its science course in 1865 and took this picture himself about 1901.

It was Garfield who uttered the famous remark that "A university is a student on one end of a log and Mark Hopkins on the other," suitable praise for the famous president of Williams. One must add, however, that Hopkins, who taught philosophy, admitted that he never got beyond the first paragraph of *The Critique of Pure Reason* and couldn't understand even that. (Morris Bishop has remarked that it might have done Hopkins good to sit on one end of a log with Immanuel Kant on the other.) The nineteenth century had many brilliant teachers, as all times do. To name only a few—Longfellow, Lowell, Parkman, Willard Gibbs, William Graham Sumner— indicates the gold amidst the dross, and with such men came new fields of study. Two of the great stars appear here at their blackboards. Opposite, lecturing while casually drawing faultless diagrams of invertebrates, stands Louis Agassiz, the great Swiss naturalist who helped turn Harvard into a university. (His widow helped found Radcliffe.) His statue at Stanford fell head-first during the San Francisco earthquake of 1906, which led to a much quoted witticism ascribed to Michigan's celebrated president James Burrill Angell: "Agassiz was great in the abstract but not in the concrete."

Above is Harvard's massive mathematical intellect Benjamin Peirce with one of his—to most students—incomprehensible formulas; he was a kind of Einstein of his age, much loved, far ahead of his time and his classes. President A. Lawrence Lowell remembered his awe as a student watching Peirce labor an hour, drop his chalk, stare moodily at the long formula he had created on the blackboard, and then say very impressively, "Gentlemen, that is surely true, it is absolutely paradoxical, we can't understand it, and we don't know what it means, but we have proved it, and thereafter we know it must be the truth." There are many such tales.

Maria Mitchell, seated firmly in her Vassar observatory in the 1870's, had studied astronomy at home in Nantucket, discovered a comet in 1847, and was already famous when she lent her prestige to the new women's college.

Yale and Harvard were becoming universities, and both set up scientific schools in the 1840's. President Francis Wayland of Brown announced in 1850 that it was time for higher education to serve the practical needs of the nation: "Lands were to be surveyed, roads to be constructed, ships to be built and navigated, soils of every kind . . . were to be cultivated, manufactures were to be established . . ." Science, in a word, was to join the classics and elbow them a little aside; the age of invention, technology, and big industry was at hand. Darwin would so shake Yale that a notice is supposed to have once appeared on the door of Professor (later President) Noah Porter reading: "At 11:30 on Tuesday Professor Porter will reconcile science and religion."

The proud young gentlemen shown here are no doubt less conscious of their place in the progress of education than of their mechanical apparatus and the set of their low-crowned bowlers. It is an engineering class in Yale's Sheffield Scientific School in 1881. The beard at rear is worn by the instructor.

Arthur Diggles   R E McDonnell
Herbert Hoover   James White
SURVEYING SQUAD - STANFORD UNIVERSITY IN 1893

Science moved forward rapidly. Above is the surveying squad at Stanford in 1893, with young Herbert Hoover seated at the left. The ponderous mechanism at right is a student's thesis apparatus designed to test electric ventilating fans, at the Massachusetts Institute of Technology in 1893.

Peering into one of his instruments above is that able student of light A. A. Michelson, one among the great carload-lots of first-rank professors and scholars who were hired at the start of the University of Chicago. Though a Naval Academy graduate with no academic degree, he collected eleven honorary ones for his work on the measurement of the velocity of light. The University of Chicago, financed with the millions donated by John D. Rockefeller when he turned from oil to good works, was created almost full-blown as a modern university by an astonishing Baptist scholar and organizer, William Rainey Harper. For faculty, he raided the whole country; Michelson was one of fifteen he acquired at Clark University alone, a majority of its academic staff.

Those who dismiss Booker T. Washington, founder of Tuskegee Institute, as an Uncle Tom commit a gross libel on America's first great black educator, a man who saw that learning, and especially practical skills first, would do more to free his people than even the Union Army. By hard work, by speaking in moderation and, on the surface at least, averting his gaze from some evils of his time, he won the absolutely necessary support of philanthropic and progressive white men, including Theodore Roosevelt and the three men shown at right with him at Tuskegee's twenty-fifth anniversary in 1906. From left they are R. C. Ogden, whose "Ogden movement" helped improve southern education, black and white, in the depressed years after the Civil War; the benign then Secretary of War William Howard Taft; and Andrew Carnegie, who gave Tuskegee the giant sum (for 1903) of $600,000. The two little pairs of pictures at left and opposite are homilies made in 1899 by the noted photographer Frances Benjamin Johnston as part of a famous series on Hampton Institute, a Virginia Negro college with very similar motives and methods to Tuskegee's. Their touching contemporary captions were, left top and bottom, "The Old Folks at Home" and "A Hampton Graduate at Home." Those of the other pair read "The Old-Time Cabin" and "A Hampton Graduate's Home." They say it all.

PAIRS OF FRANCES B. JOHNSTON PHOTOGRAPHS: PLATINUM PRINTS, 7½ × 9½", COLLECTION, THE MUSEUM OF MODERN ART, GIFT OF LINCOLN KIRSTEIN

Not every college had a benefactor like Stanford or Rockefeller, nor shady walks and mellow classrooms. In the pictures at left and far left appear do-it-yourself institutions where the students are helping create the college. On Campus Day—the one at far left is in 1906—classes were suspended at the University of Washington while male faculty and students donned work clothes to improve the grounds by digging ditches, clearing brush, laying walks. Then, in those days of female enslavement, the faculty wives and women students got up a hearty meal *al fresco*. The men near the camera don't seem to have enjoyed it very much. In our other work scene, at Tuskegee, black students are not only learning the building trades but erecting another part of their own institution. Learning while building precisely combined the ideas of Booker T. Washington, who founded the institute in 1881 as his state's first normal school for training Negro teachers, almost symbolically choosing as his site a plantation abandoned after the war.

Study, the generations have learned, requires a comfortable position. At top, in 1863, John W. Sterling, left, and Clinton Conkling, stylishly robed, undertake it at Yale. (Sterling, a poor boy who walked to Yale with a carpetbag, left it fifteen million dollars.) Above, a century later, girls at Carroll College in Waukesha, Wisconsin, stomachs down, attack Orwell, Camus, Freud. How, much, one wonders, are they really absorbing?

WIDE WORLD PHOTOS

Study proceeds above at the Brandeis University student center and at right, bare feet up, in the Firestone Library at Princeton. Marx (note the work on the table) is a popular topic, certain to agitate the old graduates but very hard to read without a good deal of squirming and position shifting. The pace in Harvard's great Widener Library, at left, has overcome one somnolent scholar entirely.

HARVEY LLOYD

CHEERING SECTION

It sometimes seems in modern America that the most important thing about a college or university is its football team, its greatest heroes the gridiron stars and coaches, its reputation something determined by taking part in the big business of bowl competitions. Yet it is, in the eye of history, a very recent matter. There were almost no organized athletics before the Civil War—a little baseball, crew, some German-style gymnastics. Sport to the New England Puritans was sinful idleness, and even in the South exercise was mostly confined to the horse. The first intercollegiate "football" game, which was really more like soccer (with twenty-five men on each side), took place between Rutgers and Princeton in 1869.

In the 1870's and 1880's the modern game evolved, largely through the agency of Walter Camp, who played for Yale for six years—long before any nonsense about eligibility—then coached and set up intercollegiate rules, from the scrimmage line to signals and the eleven-man team. The game was popular almost immediately, and if one leaves out prize fighting, it inaugurated spectator sports in this country. The alumni turned out for the big games en masse, and colors for the first time had to be devised for the Big Three—Harvard, Yale, and Princeton—which, along with Pennsylvania, dominated the game until 1900. Only two players from other teams even made the first ten All-American squads from 1889 to 1898. The first westerner, C. B. Herschberger of Chicago, appears at right.

To the anguish of faculties and of critics like President Eliot of Harvard, football soon captivated the whole country. It appealed to the martial spirit. It was democratic and brought men without means or background or old names into the forefront of college life. On the other hand, in the era of the flying wedge it was so rough that in 1905 eighteen boys were killed playing it. To clean up the brutality required President Theodore Roosevelt himself, the enemy of mollycoddles, who called a conference of the Big Three to change the rules and make the game fairer. Stricter rules, protective uniforms, and new plays like the forward pass and other devisings of great coaches like A. A. Stagg of Chicago, Pop Warner of Cornell, and Knute Rockne of Notre Dame made it a faster game.

As a nation we have a habit of overdoing things. Football, and later basketball, engaged not only the enthusiasm of the students but of the alumni, the press, and the moviemakers. Giant bands, gymnast cheerleaders, and a sentimental do-or-die spirit suffused the enterprise. It became an industry, and it helped keep Old Siwash afloat. Victories won the support of legislatures. Bowls and stadia to rival the Circus Maximus went up everywhere, and corruption and professionalism inevitably followed. Players were and to this day are bought in the open market with sham "jobs" on campus, thinly disguised pay, and a double standard of marking. There are, of course, revolts against the football industry, sometimes from the faculty, sometimes from the students, but it is a long time since the day when President Andrew White of Cornell in 1873 declined a challenge to a game in Cleveland with this telegram: "I will not permit thirty men to travel four hundred miles merely to agitate a bag of wind."

Girls took to cheerleading like camp followers to armies. Rah! Rah! Team!
And an upward, revealing leap. The cheerleaders were all men at Ivy League
colleges, in the days when every student yearned desperately for victory.

Football, old style, brings us bleachers segregated by sex at Dickinson College, in Carlisle, Pennsylvania, in 1909. The boys are freshmen, possibly restricted as part of freshman-sophomore rivalry. No one remembers for sure. Below we have the Cornell-Rochester game of 1889, sans helmets, grandstands, and any protective padding. If the action looks stiff, it is because part of it at least was posed for the slow camera of photographer Seneca Roy Stoddard, who usually portrayed scenery. Cornell won the game by an astounding 120 to 0. Pop Warner, who came back to Cornell to coach in 1897, invented the single wingback, the crouch start, and the hidden-ball play. In this last low trick, wildly successful at first, the quarterback shoved a ball up into the back of another runner's jersey; the latter would lope undisturbed to the goal line, where a teammate would extract the back-packed pigskin and touch it to earth.

60

Carried away with an idea, publicity men at Notre Dame posed Rockne's famous Four Horsemen, backfield of the undefeated, untied 1924 team, on actual horses. From left they are Don Miller, Elmer Layden, Jim Crowley, and Harry Stuhldreher. The line was called the Seven Mules. Above, Ohio State loses its first Western Conference game to Indiana in 1913. Below, nature takes over abandoned Stagg Field at Chicago after President Hutchins abolished the intercollegiate sport in 1939.

All colleges abound in wonderful group pictures of immortal teams. Above is the demure Smith basketball squad of 1898 and directly below Princeton's baseball nine of 1877. Lombard University, at Galesburg, Illinois, called its aggressive basketball captain (holding the ball,

below right) The Terrible Swede. He was Carl Sandburg. At far left is Yale's greatest eleven, including A. A. Stagg (extreme left), Captain Pa Corbin (holding ball), and behind him W. W. "Pudge" Heffelfinger. Eighteen eighty-eight's season score: Yale 698, Opponents 0.

Rowing, mainly in eight-oared shells, has always been the queen of intercollegiate sports, a test of grace, precision, and stamina; although, unlike football, it makes no money for Alma Mater. Above, with a shell ready to leap forward, is the elegant boathouse and gym of the University of Wisconsin, on Lake Mendota, sometime between 1910 and 1920. At right opposite, carefully outfitted in tam-o'-shanters, is the 1895 class crew at Wellesley in their rowing barge on Lake Waban. Intercollegiate crew lives on, refreshed by occasional forays to the Henley Regatta in England and to the Olympics, but it suffered a blow this year with the cancellation of the oldest and hardest race, the four-mile grind at New London, Connecticut, between Harvard and Yale, once the great event of graduation time, attended by thousands of yachtsmen. The crowds have thinned out, and the two universities, their football eminence vanished, are short of funds.

There are, of course, other sports, as these Wisconsin co-eds of the 1920's demonstrate. The Greek ideal of individual skill rarely attracted the enthusiasm that Americans give to team efforts. Our ideal was something for everyone, like soccer, lacrosse, baseball, and hockey; and the support of lesser and intramural sports was the price football paid for its central place in the college pantheon. The reward in any major sport was the prized letter on the hero's sweater, which was sometimes turned inside out so that the magic message appeared only in modest but unmistakeable outline. The reward for the minor sports, unheeded golf and tennis, was proficiency, and it came much later in life.

What could girls do, at least in the days before Women's
Lib answered ''Everything''? Among other things, these
Stanford co-eds of the 1920's did elaborate gymnastics.

66

They could also stage a tug of war, sometimes aided by
male volunteers, as in this free-for-all intersorority match
at Washington University in St. Louis, Missouri, in 1966.

HIGH SPIRITS

Most news from the colleges seems to come in the spring, when the sap runs, and this has been true for upwards of two hundred years. The students are rioting in the streets, climbing steeples, ringing bells at illegal hours, breaking windows, assaulting statues, starting fires. In turn they have bedevilled the stagecoach, the trolley car (with that wonderful pole to pull off the wire), and the bus; it is great fun to rock a bus, especially if it is full of shrieking girls. At any college, with its inevitable clashes between town and gown, a policeman's lot is indeed not a happy one.

Wars, popular and unpopular, add fuel to the normal fires of youth as it stands on the eager but uncertain threshold of adulthood. There were Tory-patriot troubles as the Revolution drew on and clashes before the Civil War between Northern and Southern students. The Vietnam War era, with its occupations and confrontations, is only the latest example. If that has subsided, the young will not stay quiet for long.

In their innocence, the pious men of God who founded our first colleges and universities assumed that in setting up their inflexible curriculum and providing, in most cases, dormitories, they had done all that was needed. The dormitory, they believed, would provide democratic, peaceful, godly living for their charges, under the faculty's parental supervision. But youth seethes with energy and passion untempered by experience. Even piety could stir the young men to excesses, for example during the religious revivals of the early days.

The curriculum, with its deadly round of rote learning, was undemanding, and since the colleges provided little else to challenge the intellect, it was left to the students themselves to devise what have become known as extracurricular activities, for years both the ornaments and besetting sins of American college life. Debating societies appeared first, as an expression of youthful interest in politics (a subject not taught) followed by literary societies, in which it was possible to

discuss the literature one actually enjoyed. Musical groups, dramatic clubs, athletic teams, student publications, were also invented by the students themselves, but their most visible creation, beginning in the early 1820's and 30's were the Greek-letter fraternities, of which further hereafter.

It is hard to disapprove of the high spirits of the young, which are creative as well as destructive. Where faculties and administrations abdicated, they stepped in with their extracurricular activities to shatter the quiet ways of the old-fashioned colleges and project them into the hurly-burly of modern American life. And as one old Harvard tutor put it, "Wild colts often make good horses."

K.S.K.
Down where the Wurzberger flows.

Exuberance at one's own devilish ways lies just below the surface in hundreds of college photographs; for example, the two jolly Yale men of about 1880 opposite, and the Knights of the Skull and Crossbones at Westminster College, Missouri, above.

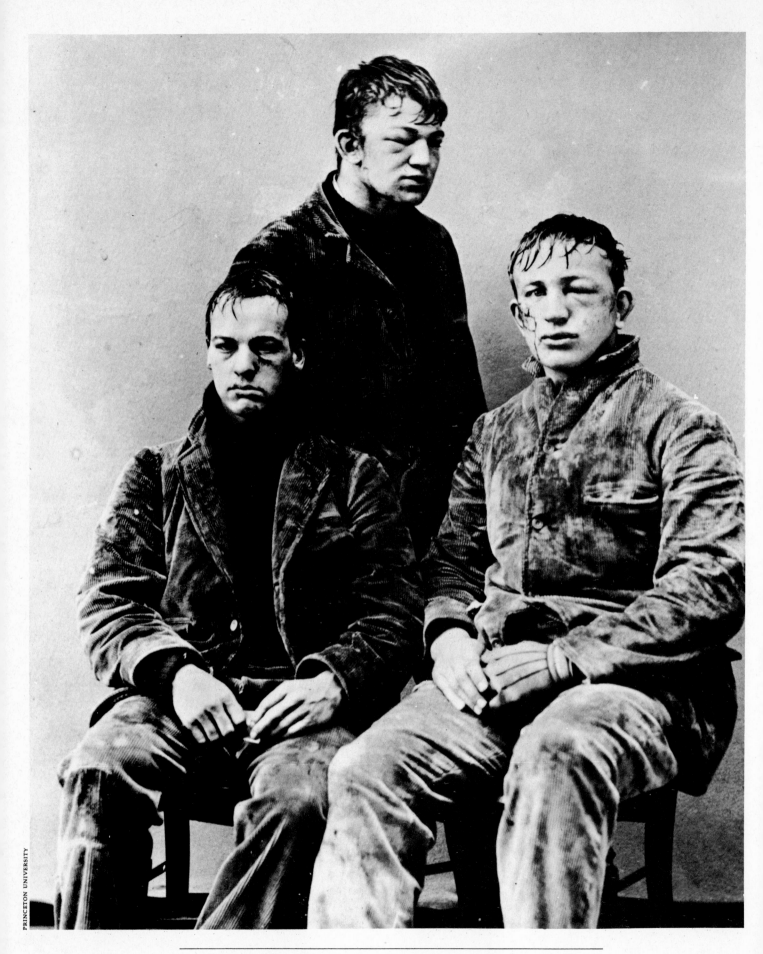

Captured malefactors? No, Princeton freshmen of the class of 1895 after an impromptu brawl with the sophomores. At left, D. R. James, a future banker; at center, John P. Poe, grandnephew of the poet.

"Sophomores and freshmen," wrote James Bryce, putting a good face on harsh facts, "have a whimsical habit of meeting one another in dense masses and trying which can push the other aside on the stairs or path. This is called 'rushing.'" Testing the manhood of the new members of the group is a custom as old as the most primitive societies, whether expressed in individual hazing or mass mayhem like that taking place above at the University of Rochester (New York) in 1915. Such whimsies produced so much injury around the country that most rushes were suppressed in later years. Football filled the vacuum.

Humiliation and heavy-handed humor for generations characterized admission into campus clubs and fraternities, although, as sacred mysteries, they were very infrequently photographed. Those shown on these pages are, at the left, ritual paddling at Montana University in the 1918 era; a Sigma Chi initiation (above) staged at the University of Iowa sometime around 1910; and another Iowa ceremony of the same ilk and period (opposite). Recent college generations, exposed to Freud and psychology and democratic ideas, have turned their backs on fraternity mummeries, if not on the institution itself.

Greek-letter fraternities and sororities are peculiar to the

United States (and Canada); they stand outside the stated organization of universities much as political parties are outside the Constitution. Excluding Phi Beta Kappa, born in 1776 but soon changed into an honor society, the oldest ones, like Kappa Alpha, Sigma Phi, Alpha Delta Phi, Psi Upsilon, and Beta Theta Pi, date to the 1820's and 30's. They were set up in reaction to the bleakness of dormitory life and to satisfy yearnings for distinction. Their influence, for good and bad, was enormous. The anguish and emotional energy which were expended on them by those taken in and those excluded seems, looking back over the years, both incalculable and ludicrous.

That's Katharina, at left, in *The Taming of the Shrew*, her finger pointing across the page and the years at a spindly Lady Macbeth. Katharina is being played in 1912 at Yale by the late William C. Bullitt, first U.S. ambassador to the Soviet Union, and Lady Macbeth at Harvard by Henry Cabot Lodge the elder, the eminent senator and historian, in the Hasty Pudding Club play in 1867. All-male college theatre was one of the most successful parts of the "extracurriculum." And besides, there was nothing like mincing about in skirts and wigs to bring down the house. James Stewart, class of 1932, leans against a tree while wooing Harry H. Dunham, class of 1933, in a production of the Princeton Triangle Club. For years the club was one of the most brilliant undergraduate theatre companies in the country. Other members of the same era included the noted director Joshua Logan and the actor José Ferrer. As the years wore on, the good Ivy League dramatic clubs began to write and compose all their own plays and musicals.

The charming trio of photographs opposite, from the scrapbooks of the Hasty Pudding Club, are all of the same three men, and in the same order. First they appear as ballerinas in

1863, and finally, fifty years on (to echo Harrow's song), with the original photograph. The three, who all became distinguished doctors, were, from left, John Warren, Amos Mason, and George Shattuck. Since the beginning in 1844, Pudding dramatics have called on such stars as Phillips Brooks, Senator Lodge, Justice Oliver Wendell Holmes, Owen Wister, William Randolph Hearst, George Santayana, J. P. Morgan, Robert Benchley, Robert E. Sherwood, Jack Lemmon, Archibald Cox, Alan Jay Lerner, one more Benchley, and *two* more Lodges.

Greek plays were popular in the West, especially at Beloit College in Wisconsin under the aegis of the noted Professor Theodore Lyman Wright. This was an all-male *Electra,* in 1896, translated by Wright's class.

If some sang for fun in white glee clubs of the times, the famous Jubilee Singers of Fisk University sang for their supper or, more precisely, to keep the school out of threatened bankruptcy. A Union veteran, George L. White, teaching at the new college, had organized a choir out of his newly freed students; a fund-raising tour of the country was laid on in 1871. The repertory was strictly classical music and the tour a failure until the singers, on request, did a few spirituals, which were an instant success. And with these old black plantation melodies, which they privately disdained, the Fisk Jubilee Singers made a triumphal tour of America and Europe. Perhaps their most famous number is still remembered to have been "Didn't My Lord Deliver Daniel? (And Why Not Every Man?)."

Fisk had a strange beginning in an abandoned army barracks in Nashville, Tennessee. The founder, Clinton Bowen Fisk, a former Union general, set out to teach "young men and women irrespective of color." Fisk was also an ardent prohibitionist who once ran for President on that ticket. But he had better luck with learning than with the saloon interests, for Fisk, together with Howard, has become one of the most successful private Negro colleges.

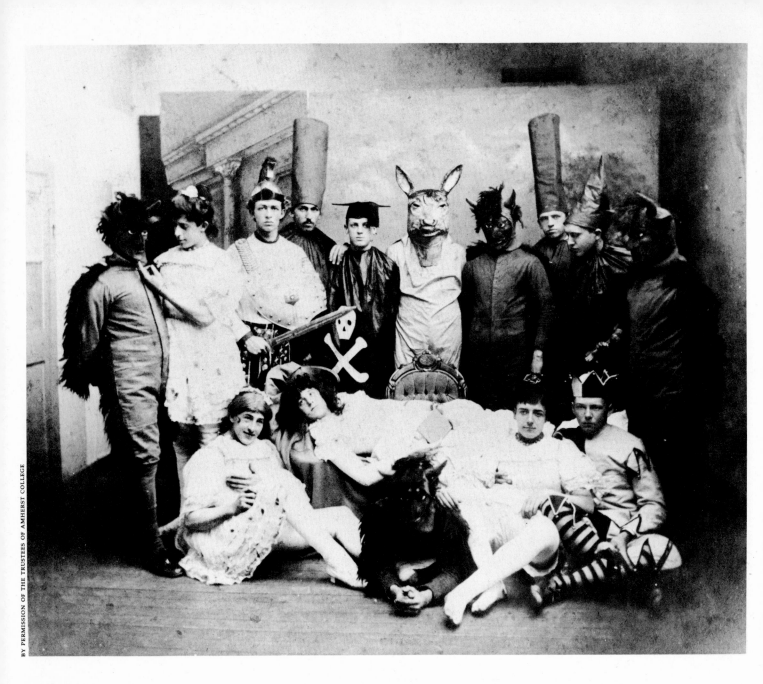

Once their time is past, ceremonies and protests are so quickly forgotten that no one can remember exactly what they were about, a thought that might chill today's Mark Rudds and Jane Fondas. Above, for instance, we have an obscure celebration of "The Burial of Mathematics," elaborate but sedate, at Amherst in 1880. Was the course over? Opposite above at Harvard in the 1880's, no longer identifiable students either condemn compulsory chapel or celebrate its abolition, which came in 1886. "Godless Harvard!" exclaimed many at this frightening novelty. At barely more godly Yale (below) a better remembered trick is pulled in 1902 on the hatchet-wielding enemy of the liquor traffic, Carry Nation. A group of wags at Yale had invited her to visit them at Mory's, the refreshment center for the celebrated Whiffenpoofs, and had a group picture taken for the press. Into her hand these Greeks bearing gifts retouched a cigarette and into her glass of water what looks like the foam on a glass of beer. She does seem to be blowing smoke rings. Poor earnest Carry had thought they were all such nice young men.

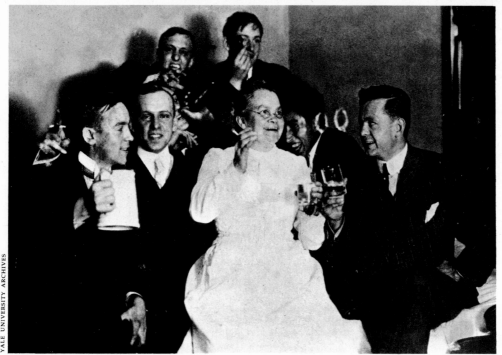

82

The skeleton joke works its magic in 1923 for an outing of the Reed College biology club, pro-digally equipped with bones. *Venit mors velociter,/Rapit nos atrociter,/Nemini parcetur,* goes one verse of "*Gaudeamus.*" But no one of college age really believes death will come for him.

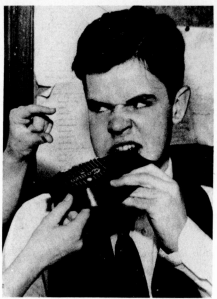

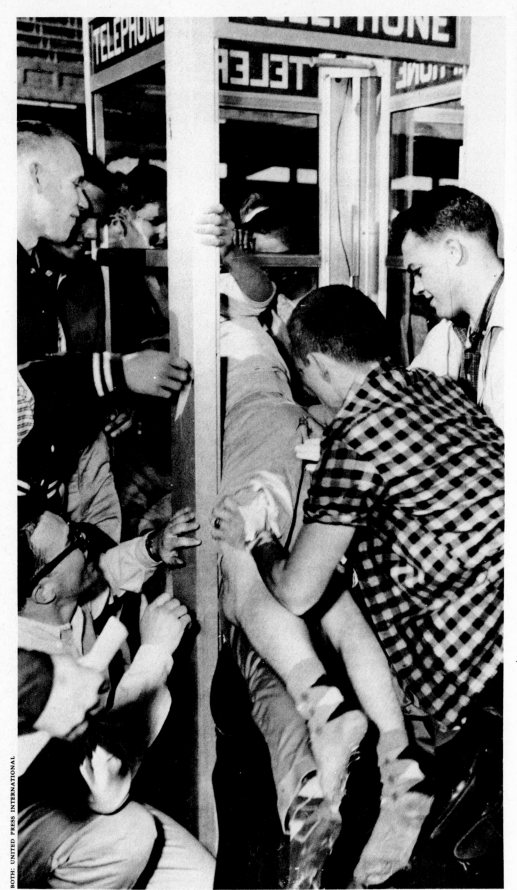

We come here to some landmark events in the history of higher education, all of which took place in April or May, which is more significant than the years involved. At left members of Iota Kappa Epsilon at Creighton University in Omaha, Nebraska, are shown stuffing twenty-four scholars into an upright phone booth; however, men at Oklahoma bested them with thirty-three. Above is a University of Chicago junior, John Patrick, consuming a nourishing meal of two and a half phonograph records, including "Deep Purple" and "Who's Sorry Now?" in the year 1939.

UNITED PRESS INTERNATIONAL

The scene now moves on to Harvard for the bowl event, so to speak, in the 1939 goldfish classic, where sophomore Irving Clark, left, is downing his record of twenty-four live, wriggling examples of genus *Carassius auratus*. "They're kind of bitter, but they go down easy," was the champ's sole, possibly misquoted comment. At right, like knights of old bearing their ladies' handkerchiefs, panty-raiders of 1952 at Northwestern University, a temple of learning in Illinois, display their trophies. Below, for 1974, we have streakers at the University of Florida; they are fully integrated. Women naturally cannot be excluded either. At Carleton College in Minnesota, Laura Barton, eighteen, wearing only a ski mask, sneakers, and red, white, and blue socks, "streaked" a theatre. Laura seems to have lost her beau as a result but observed philosophically (to the Associated Press) that "anyone who gets that embarrassed wouldn't be worth dating, anyhow."

UNITED PRESS INTERNATIONAL

WIDE WORLD PHOTOS

SIGNS OF THE TIMES

One hot summer day during the American Revolution a Harvard student emerged from a long afternoon in the library and was astonished to learn that, quite nearby, the Battle of Bunker Hill had been raging. It is a kind of detachment scarcely conceivable in our own tumultuous twentieth century, when the signs of the times are inescapable. In the age of mass communications it is inevitable that the colleges and universities have become a kind of distorted mirror of the world outside.

The strenuous "manliness" exemplified by Theodore Roosevelt, the glamour of the doughboy training at Plattsburgh, the disillusioned letdown of the 1920's, the bitterness of the Great Depression—all found exaggerated echoes among the young. Naturally they were in turn more strenuous, more eager to get "over there," more beautiful and more damned, more depressed. And to pick a later era at random, when the nation slumbered through the Eisenhower years, the so-called Silent Generation was so conformist that it became famous, when job-hunting, for its obsessive interest—at age twenty-two or twenty-three—in the pension benefits offered by prospective employers.

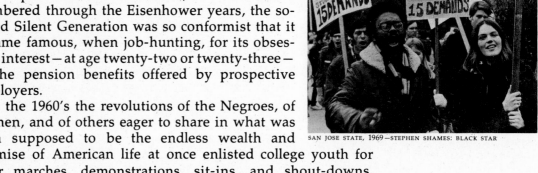

SAN JOSE STATE, 1969—STEPHEN SHAMES: BLACK STAR

In the 1960's the revolutions of the Negroes, of women, and of others eager to share in what was then supposed to be the endless wealth and promise of American life at once enlisted college youth for their marches, demonstrations, sit-ins, and shout-downs. Youth has very little patience with opposing views. As a child tests the firmness of its parents' discipline, what seemed to be a whole generation suddenly enthusiastic for violence, for drugs, for outrageous behavior, deliberately tried the temper of university authorities. And the surrogate parent was flabby. Surrender was often abject and instantaneous, with faculty members joining the demonstrations; rules, whether for dress, attendance, prescribed study of any kind, sexual conduct, went out the window. The supposedly powerful educational Establishment, which was really not to blame anyway for the slave trade, the atom bomb, poverty, or Vietnam, proved to be a mountain of jelly, and one suspects the young revolutionists were secretly disappointed by their easy victory.

Higher education itself entered the fray in what a sober Carnegie Commission report called "grave trouble." Weakened financially, unsure of what to teach, overburdened by post-World War II expansion, faced with the sudden problem of keeping the light of knowledge burning in the face of "universal access," the universities were tempting targets.

We are always assured in such cases that the rebels are merely extremists, and very few in number. But nearly all the work of history is done by small minorities. Indeed it is minorities that give any era, on campus or off, its mood and style. As we inspect a few recent college generations on the next few pages, it might be well to ask ourselves how many gilded youths of the 1920's actually owned Stutz Bearcats, how many of the next wave really swallowed goldfish, and how many girls were in cold fact seduced in rumble seats.

SAN FRANCISCO, 1964—
UNITED PRESS INTERNATIONAL

86

In June, 1969, a visiting Sweet Briar girl at Princeton encounters a lingering sign of old-time delicacy. That fall Old Nassau joined the rush of colleges taking both sexes and facing the problem of the totally co-ed bathroom.

SMITH COLLEGE

UNIVERSITY OF WISCONSIN

CHARLES PHELPS CUSHING STUDIO

There are as many images of the 1920's as there were creative interpreters of the ivied halls of that far-off time. Some find theirs in Scott Fitzgerald's disillusioned sophisticates, some in the world-weary hedonism of Edna St. Vincent Millay's famous quatrain about the candle that burns at both its ends. You can turn to the warm but callow figure of Harold Lloyd as "The Freshman," or you can pull out all the stops and remember flaming youth in the cartoons of John Held, Jr., populated with "sheiks" in slick hair and coonskin coats drinking bathtub gin and dancing the Charleston all night with their "shebas," hot numbers in short hair and shorter dresses with supposedly deplorable mating habits. It is difficult if not impossible to recreate this last, most popular image, we must admit, in real photographs of real colleges. Above we do have a fine group of Smith girls clowning with a vintage Ford station wagon and opposite a genuine rolled (*flesh-colored!*) stocking at an otherwise fairly innocuous fraternity barn dance at the University of Wisconsin in 1927. We know only that the Fitzgerald-style collegians at right above are singing on a station platform. Is it *Aura Lee, Show Me the Way to Go Home,* or *Who?* As for a good coonskin on a real student, we could not find one.

What happened to flaming youth? The fires cooled in the Crash and the Depression. In what seemed more like a century than a decade since the Jazz Age campuses were as peaceful as this idyllic scene at Rollins College in Florida in 1940.

Tradition was steady, as they say in Wall Street, at the women's colleges in the late thirties, with hoop rollers at Bryn Mawr (above) and a "court of beauty" at Mount Holyoke. But in a few years the beauties would be Wacs and war wives.

WE PLEDGE OURSELVES— We will not support the United States in any War!

Until fairly modern times wars and their attendant adventures were popular on American campuses. Opposite, the Great Hall of the College of the City of New York plays barracks to thousands thirsting to get to France in 1918. But by 1934 the banner above more accurately reflected the pacifist and radical views at C.C.N.Y., then sometimes called "The Little Red Schoolhouse," at least before the Hitler-Stalin pact. Below, a much angrier generation later, we have anti-Vietnam War demonstrators parading at Berkeley, California, in 1965.

The end of the war, during which college enrollments had shrunk, filled the campuses with returning soldiers, many of them married and playing their role in the "baby boom" that would so pack the colleges in the later sixties. The domestic scene below is at Dartmouth. The fifties came on with their curiously conservative, tradition-loving Silent Generation. There was never such a time for football, fraternities, and formal dances, especially in the so-called Big Ten and other western universities, as in the scene at right at Wisconsin. Opposite we have another straight-arrow crew-cut group, dressed to the nines, singing away at Brown.

1955 HOMECOMING QUEEN

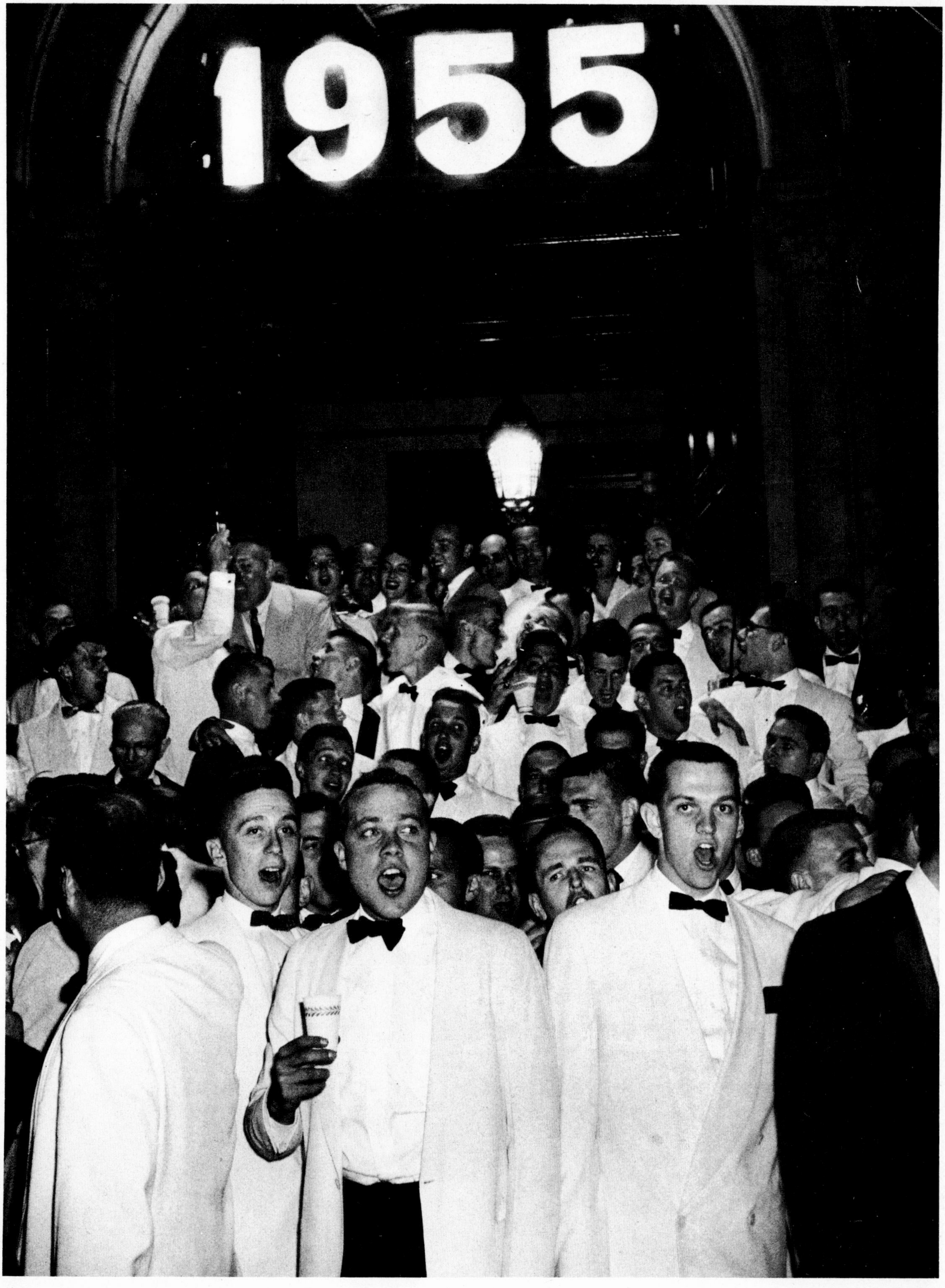

ELLIOTT ERWITT: MAGNUM

No matter what the obstacles set before it in the sterner past, college romance has managed to find a way, as with the innocent and unidentified couple below, communing with the view and each other atop Mount Holyoke, Massachusetts, in 1909. Romance, or at least a relation between the sexes, is now about as overt as it was once shy and covert. It is even in the curriculum, with no topic barred, although one may wonder whether peeking into the windows of the temple of the sacred mysteries is not after all more diverting than simply smashing the door down. We cannot imagine what our sedate couple would have thought of the scenes above on these pages.

Parietal rules, although constantly changing, were once strict, especially when it came to boys and girls visiting in one another's living quarters at college: no girls upstairs in fraternities, all boys out of the girls' rooms by such and such an hour, doors to be left ajar by so many inches. This long, losing battle for propriety suffered from vacation mores, of which the scene during the annual spring swarming at Fort Lauderdale, Florida (far left), was a celebrated example. The whole system collapsed at once, like the Wonderful One Horse Shay, in the late sixties. At center left, Barnard girls move into Columbia dormitories, and in the next picture, at Harvard, even the citadel of the bathroom has fallen. The administrations threw in the towel. At newly co-educational Vassar, a sophomore related in 1973 that her house president had put it this way: "Smoke whatever you like, sleep with whomever you like, just watch the noise." At least correct grammar survived.

UNIVERSITY OF MASSACHUSETTS AT AMHERST

What is the matter with college education in our times? Let us not all answer at once, but instead listen to the imposing figure at the right, Columbia University's famous president for forty-four years (1901–45), Nicholas Murray Butler, attacking the "wholly false philosophy" of "Progressive" educators:

These new and numerous Philistines are concerned with displacing discipline for indiscipline, scholarship for deftly organized opportunities for ignorance, thoroughness for superficiality, and morals for impulsive and appetitive conduct.

When he said that in the thirties, Butler, defender of the classics and of a gentlemanly view of education in general, branded all he saw before him the "New Barbarism." What, one cannot help wondering, would he have thought of the scene at Columbia some thirty years later, in the Black May of 1968, as recalled in the other pictures on these pages?

Remember that it was the year of the assassination of Robert Kennedy and Martin Luther King, the year of the bloody Democratic Convention in Chicago, the year of Czechoslovakia, the year when escalation in Vietnam drove Lyndon Johnson out of politics, a year of tragedy and malaise. Hating the war, fearing the draft, already caught up in its own revolution, youth in that violent spring responded with outright nationwide rebellion against Alma Mater. That it was inappropriate to indict institutions that were struggling to bring in the minorities, that seemed to accommodate to every demand, indeed that were often providing scholarships for the very leaders of the rebellions, made no apparent difference. Surrender, in fact, seemed only to aggravate the attacks.

At Columbia five buildings were seized, held for six days, and vandalized—even to the irreplaceable papers of professors and the office of President Grayson Kirk. With storm-trooper tactics the S.D.S. (ironically, "Students for a Democratic Society") and the Student Afro-American Society held faculty members prisoner, effectively closed down the university, and issued various demands, including one for that painless modern martyrdom called amnesty. Eventually a thousand tough New York cops dispossessed the occupiers in a melee during which 130 were hurt and 698 arrested.

With a kind of sullen peace returned to the politically and socially fragmented American campus, Chris Parks, a young former co-editor of the newspaper at the University of Michigan, looked the new situation over:

Back then, it was enough if you were under thirty, wore blue jeans and opposed the war. Now we have to know if you're male or female, black or white, gay or straight, liberal, radical, Socialist, Communist, or labor committee. Or maybe you're into one of a hundred gurus, meditation groups or other odd mystic orders.

For once, we suspect, words would have failed Nicholas Murray Butler.

BROWN BROTHERS

Nicholas Murray Butler at Class Day exercises, 1920

ST. CLAIR BOURNE: BLACK STAR

Black students, self-segregated, occupying an office

Columbia occupiers and the fuzz, 1968

A lady makes an entrance

Police ready to retake a building

Mark Rudd, maximum leader of the Columbia occupation, favors an eager press with an interview. ''My son the revolutionary!'' exclaimed his middle-class mother proudly.

Since the struggles of the late sixties at Columbia and other unhappy campuses, the war has ended and an uneasy peace emerged. The graffiti outlast the rebellions, as above at Harvard, but the students seem to be back at work.

A FEW LAST WORDS

Commencement: Much marching, or at least shuffling, about the campus in unaccustomed rented gown, feeling faintly ridiculous in the mortar board; at some magic moment the tassels are to be switched in unison to the other side by the new bachelors of arts; professors suddenly gorgeous in their bright hoods; a sudden influx of parents, whose conduct must be watched narrowly; old grads in comic reunion costumes (could they ever be *us*?); goodbyes; future plans, and over all the drone of speakers from the dais—the class orator, whose words are best lost to history, and the Distinguished Speaker addressing himself to the desirability of "character" and "service" in an outside world where opportunity beckons. At my college I recall a last bellowing chorus of "Bright College Years" set to the crashing strains of "The Watch on the Rhine," ending in the words, "For God, for country, and for Yale," often laughed at as a fine example of anticlimax; and I remember being sad that it was all over.

Still at Yale, but over three decades and Lord knows how many revolutions later: here are some probably unrepresentative quotations from recent Yale class-book entries in which three graduates themselves note their activities or interests. A male graduate passed the precious hours of youth, he explains: "Listening to Dylan ([during years] 2,3,4); throwing football (1–4); being bored (1–4); being horny (1–4); getting stoned (2,3,4); eating and sleeping (1–4); wanting to leave (1–4). Future occupation: teacher at all levels, mailman, truck driver, hobo, cowboy. . ." Another young man, a philosophy-psychology major: "S.D.S. (1,2); Ananda Marga Yoga Society (3,4). Occupation: Person. All hail the one cosmic mind Jai Baba."

In this interesting mixture of college humor and confessional we also find a young woman who lists her interests as "Naked breakfast (3); nude swimming at Payne Whitney Gym, interpersonal perception (3,4); Future occupation: Catatonic, etc. Even the educators must be educated!"

Perhaps there is something to that last gratuitous remark; it is hard to escape the conclusion that somewhere in the last few decades the people in charge of American higher education have lost their way. Beset by egalitarianism, distracted by every current mood and catchword, deceived by hopes of perpetual affluence, many educators—not all, not all—find themselves in the mid seventies simply housekeeping a drifting giant, waiting for a change in the weather. As for the students, is "Jai Baba" (whatever that is) any improvement on Joe College? Could or would such a generation, a quarter-century hence, support Yale's next big endowment drive?

One cannot read very much in the history of education without being unbearably moved by the sense of mission that motivated the builders of our universities, believers in steady improvement in the condition of man. One cannot, of course, go back, but life does move in cycles; great educators may reappear. The weather does change, although it is best to keep one's hands busy while waiting.

Caps and gowns linger on as badges of academe, however faces are modified, from John Burroughs getting a Litt.D. at Yale in 1910 and the Columbia B.A. of 1968 (both opposite) to the girl above *reading* (tch!) her valedictory remarks at Chicago.

The academic procession slowly shuffles by at Harvard in 1915, led by President A. Lawrence Lowell, head bowed, and such other "relics and types of our ancestors' worth" as Bishop William Lawrence (second row) and white-bearded Senator Henry Cabot Lodge (third row).

The old-time commencement called for a distinguished speaker to urge youth onward to its duties to the country and the golden future. If you had President Theodore Roosevelt, shown here making a joke at the University of Washington in Seattle in 1903, you got a rouser.

106

Throughout most of the twentieth century the alumnus, and to a lesser extent his feminine counterpart, has been expected to lend a note of humor and nostalgia to commencement. He appears in a comic costume, struggles to remember the Christian names of his balding classmates, and wanders about the campus seeking familiar landmarks. These three groups of paraders at Columbia—the "Orientals" of 1903, the "Romans" of 1911, the chain gang of 1910—are familiar types. "Class spirit" is stronger in America than back in England, although the American alumni play a smaller part in university governance than they do there. In general, these old parties are assumed, somewhat incorrectly, to be totally irrelevant Babbitts whose out-of-date ideas must be ignored, while at the same time they must be conjured into financing the new whatever-it-is and relieving the current—the always current—financial deficit of Alma Mater.

At graduation, one might say, the faculty gives you its last long glare; this is Stevens Institute of Technology, at Hoboken, New Jersey, about 1915. Perhaps they are only squinting into the sun.

This is the ultimate moment—graduation—at Vassar College about 1900, which has grown into a kind of secular sacrament of American life. What did the valedictorian say? What were you thinking? Does anyone really remember?

For those who would care to pursue further the many subjects touched on, or for that matter simply passed by, in the modest compass of this picture book, the following volumes are particularly recommended, among others we read or consulted: *The American College and University: A History*, by Frederick Rudolph, Alfred A. Knopf, New York, 1962; *The College Charts Its Course*, by R. Freeman Butts, McGraw-Hill Book Company, New York, 1939; *The State Universities and Democracy*, by Allan Nevins, University of Illinois Press, Urbana, 1962; *The Higher Learning in America: A Reassessment*, by Paul Woodring, McGraw-Hill Book Company, New York, 1968; *Early Cornell, 1865–1900*, by Morris Bishop, Cornell University Press, Ithaca, New York, 1962; *The Gentle Puritan, A Life of Ezra Stiles, 1727–1795*, by Edmund S. Morgan, Yale University Press, New Haven, Connecticut, 1962; *The Art of Teaching*, by Gilbert Highet, Random House, New York, 1950; *Alma Mater: The Gothic Age of the American College*, by Henry Seidel Canby, Farrar & Rinehart, New York, 1936; *The Academic Revolution*, by Christopher Jencks and David Riesman, Doubleday and Company, New York, 1968; and *Priorities for Action: Final Report of the Carnegie Commission on Higher Education*, McGraw-Hill Book Company, New York, 1973. The authors of these books, which are all highly readable and often inspired, are not to be blamed for any errors into which we may have fallen here in the course of that kind of shoplifting called research; this author's obvious prejudices are not necessarily those of any of the writers cited nor of his kind, patient, and open-minded collaborators, who are listed on page 10. Finally we commend to the reader a look back at his or her own class book, if it can be found. It will prove an absorbing, prophetic, and nostalgic work, just as anyone else's will turn out to be callow and jejune.

MOOD: ELEGIAC. LOCATION? UNKNOWN. PICTURE: BROWN BROTHERS.

"So the boat glides pleasantly along, with little to mark what is really happening, and when the farther shore is reached, the transit, in retrospect, seems short indeed. But the passengers are not the boys who came aboard, for although they have the same names and the same class numbers, they are quite different people."

— A. Lawrence Lowell